Pitman New Era
Shorthand

Workbook 2

Anniversary Edition

GW00535594

Pitman New Era Shorthand

Workbook 2

Anniversary Edition

B W Canning

Pitman New Era Shorthand

ADDISON WESLEY LONGMAN LIMITED
Edinburgh Gate, Harlow
Essex CM20 2JE, England
and Associated Companies throughout the world

First published 1988
Reprinted 1989, 1993
Reprinted by Pitman Publishing 1995
Reprinted by Longman Group Limited 1996

British Library Cataloguing in Publication Data
A catalogue entry for this title is available from the British Library.

ISBN 0 273 02903 7

Library of Congress Cataloging-in-Publication Data
A catalog entry for this title is available from the Library of Congress.

Printed in Singapore

Contents

Introduction

The material in *Workbooks 1* and *2* is to be used with *Pitman New Era Shorthand Anniversary Edition*. *Workbook 1* covers units 1–12 and *Workbook 2* continues up to unit 20.

Once you have completed Units 1–5 of the *Anniversary Edition*, you will need to use these *Workbooks*. The exercises will enable you to improve your speed, phrasing and accuracy in writing Pitman Shorthand.

Use the exercises to look again at the theory which you have just studied and to practise the short forms, words and phrases which you have learnt. To hear, see and write the outlines at the same time is the best method of improving your shorthand; it also helps you to recognise and remember the outlines.

For extra practice, get someone to dictate the exercises to you or make your own cassette recording. Always check the outlines you have written against the printed shorthand and drill any which are incorrect. Drilling an outline means writing it again and again until it can be written without thinking.

Each section is divided up as follows:

Phrases

a Read through each group of phrases as quickly as you can. Refer to the longhand key if necessary. Repeat the reading until you can read each outline without hesitation.

b Write the phrases from dictation, or copy the exercise in your notebook, writing quickly and accurately. Say the words to yourself as you write. Practise each phrase two or three times.

c Then turn to the key and write the phrases from the longhand. Check your outlines against the printed shorthand.

Short forms

It is essential to know each short form and be able to write the outline without hesitating.

a Read each sentence until you can do so fluently.

b Find the short forms in the sentence and write them down.

c Take down the sentences from dictation, or turn to the key and write them in shorthand from the longhand.

d Check your shorthand carefully against the printed shorthand, making sure that the position of each outline is correct. Remember that, if possible, each short form in a phrase should take its correct position.

e When all the sentences have been practised, try to take them down from dictation at 60 words a minute (wam).

Blank line dictation drills

a Read through the shorthand as quickly as you can. Check the key if any outline causes you to hesitate.

b Complete the first of the blank lines from dictation, or, saying the words to yourself as you write them, copy the shorthand on the first of the two blank lines. Write as fast as possible, but make sure your outlines are accurate and neat. Use a stopwatch, if available, to check your speed and to see how many words you can write in one minute. Then check your outlines with the printed shorthand.

c Now use the second blank line to write the outlines again at a higher speed. Try to take the passage from dictation at, say, 80 wam. This will help to build your speed.

d Finally, write the passage again in your own notebook without the help of the printed shorthand. Try to take this down from dictation at about 70 wam. Check your outlines with the printed shorthand.

Theory check

a Take these words from dictation, or write the shorthand outlines in your notebook, making sure you have put in all the vowel signs.

b Check your outlines with those given in the key. Drill any which caused you to hesitate, writing them again and again until you have mastered them.

Free dictation

This can be used as an unprepared test for dictation, or read through and prepared as with the previous material. Type your shorthand notes for transcription practice.

Section 9
Units 1–13

Key: page 50

Phrases

1

2

3

4

5

6

Short forms

1

2

3

4

5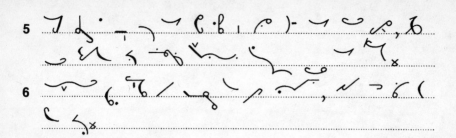

6

Blank line dictation drills
1 Problems of installing new machines

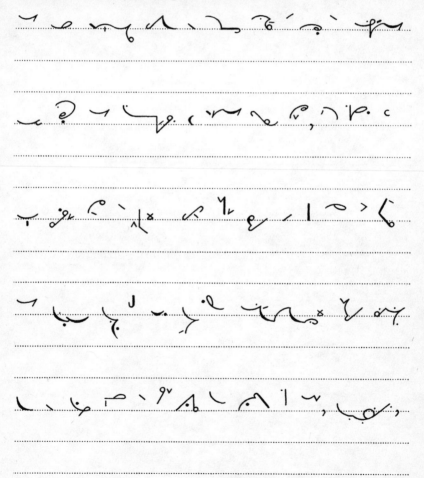

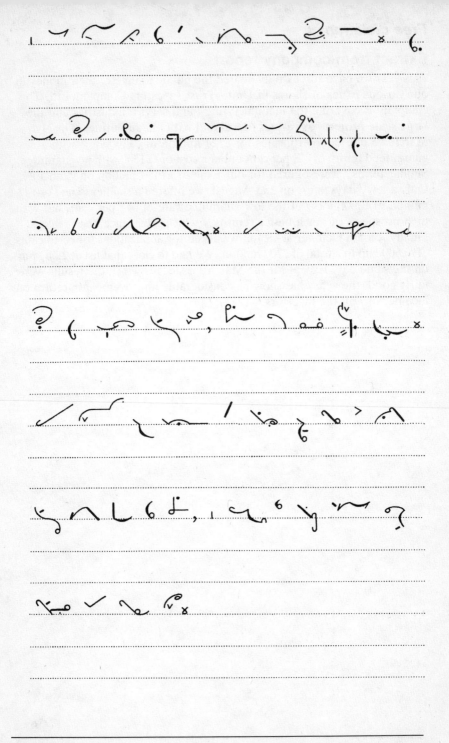

Free dictation

Extract from company report

This year we have successfully invited the public to invest / their money in our various issues of shares in Unit / Trust Investors Company Ltd. This company is covering the manufacturing / and service industries and the large scale projects of various / local and national authorities. On 21st March we offered / certificates for £124 million in / £1000 lots with a guaranteed return of / $7\frac{1}{4}$ per cent but at a cost of / £1500 with no guarantee. Similar terms / were offered for our issue of £165 / million on 22nd July. Only a few / days later, on 2nd August, we offered a smaller issue / of £42 million in £2000 lots / at the low guarantee rate of $6\frac{1}{2}$ / per cent, but with high prospects of much better returns, / which have since been realised. Finally, on 5th October at / 9 am, we asked for applications for certificates of / £5000 up to a total of £20 / million. We had to close that list at 2.30 / pm on the same day. Except for the March / issue, for which the results were fairly good, the year / has shown a considerable improvement in return on income for / all the investors. *(223)*

2 Letter about high quality paper

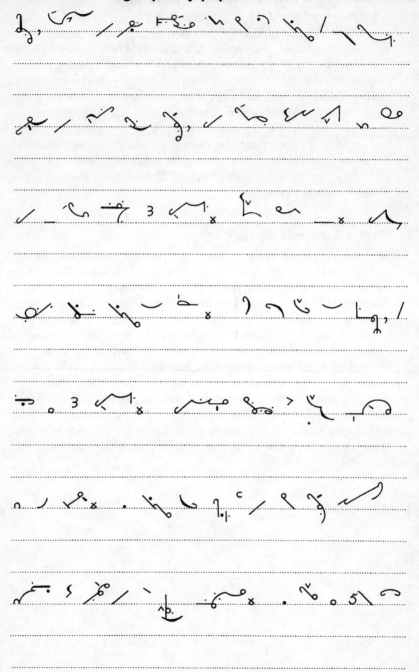

2   Improving a firm's business potential

We-are well aware of-the magnitude of-the problems we face and-
we-shall fail to accomplish-the commercial aims of-our organisation
unless we secure better accommodation both for office and works staff.
Our transport must-be self-contained and-we-must no-longer rely
on-private firms as-we-have-done in-the-past. We-shall instruct our
Accounts-Department to transfer-the necessary funds for
replacing-the old fleet of vans which-we inherited more-than ten
years-ago. We-shall also run a close check on-the commission of any
unnecessary or time-wasting procedures due to-the thoughtlessness of
departmental managers. The committee organising this-will hold-the
first of-its meetings in-January, and-we already-have a report giving
details of initial savings.   *(131)*

3   Firm's successful recovery

The announcement of-our-business achievements in-the year just past
will-be welcome to-the majority-of our staff who know of-the liabilities
we faced at-the-beginning of-the period. However-the possibility
remains that, through carelessness or some-other cause, a minority
of-our staff-contributed to-this situation. It-was a time of hardship
for-us all, and our indebtedness to-many of-our creditors was a
cause-of-concern. Our current success is due particularly to-our
technological advances. Today-the new biological research-
department is becoming a leader in-its field. In-addition, the
rate-of-interest on-the four-hundred-million pounds we had to-raise
has-been cut by-government aid to 5 per-cent-per-annum. We-shall
look to-the future and to increased income from our new ventures.
Our next meeting will-be held at 1430 hours on Tuesday 23rd
July.   *(155)*

Theory check

1 ....

6 ....

2 ....

7 ....

3 ....

8 ....

4 ....

9 ....

5 ....

10 ....

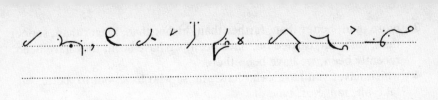

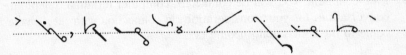

3 Memorandum to office staff

(a)

3 more than, better than, farther than, higher than, longer than, sooner than, carry on, carried on, have been, we have been, they have been, recently been, we have been there.

4 which have, you have, who have, those who have, out of, better off, take off, range of, type of.

5 I am confident, you will be contacted, computer terminal, telephone conversation, for your consideration, in connection with the, I have come to the conclusion, income tax.

Short forms

1 I-consider that instruction in commercial subjects is an important part-of-the curriculum in-this course. *(17)*

2 In-the-circumstances the government-department welcomes-the opportunity to advertise-the introduction of-these concepts to-the public. *(19)*

3 All advertisements are governed by a regular code-of practice and-the governing body of-the advertising industry looks to individuals to-call-attention to any breaches of-the code. *(30)*

4 It-seems-probable that if-his appointment becomes-confirmed in-the next-few-months the prospect for our manufacturing industry is good. *(22)*

5 It-is-not sufficient just to-read-the introduction to-this manual; it-is recommended that-the instructions should-be read in full by each individual student before using-the-computer. *(31)*

6 It-is instructive to compare-the figures for last-year, when our trading circumstances were so different, with-those for-the-present year, and it-is becoming clear that-the differences show-the benefits of-the changes in taxation. *(39)*

7 A regular advertisement in-our local newspaper for a week or-two will-probably avoid the inconvenience of telling individual customers about-the new sales-policy, which-we-hope they-will welcome. *(32)*

Blank line dictation drills

1 Trading results investigation

A company-committee set-up to-reconsider its trading results for-the past three-years has decided to-call in a consultant to investigate this-matter on-their behalf. The recommendations will-be put forward at a meeting of-the-committee, and a majority vote will-be taken. In-our-own self-interest, this should-be carried-out as-quickly-as-possible. *(62)*

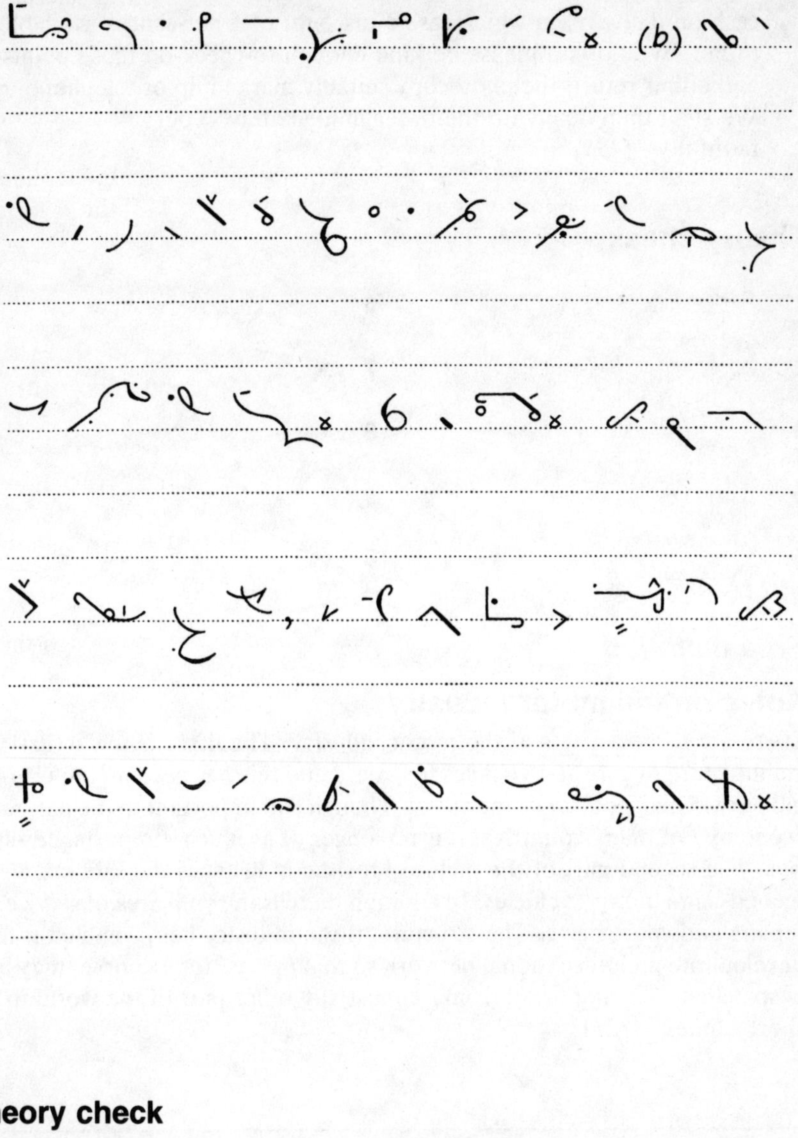

Theory check

Write the following in shorthand. Each outline should be written in its correct position, and all vowels should be inserted.

1 remains
2 moments
3 training
4 assistant
5 student

6 fence
7 accident
8 routine
9 bargain
10 wanted

cash on-delivery, in-which-case a discount of 5 per-cent is available to-her. Would-you please be kind enough to-check-on these points and either return-the photocopy suitably marked up or telephone-us? We-shall then deal-with-the order immediately. Yours-faithfully *(135)*

Theory check

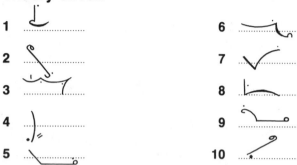

1

6

2

7

3

8

4

9

5

10

Free dictation

Notes on the motor industry

There are three aspects of the motor industry. The first / is the actual manufacture of cars and vehicles for sale, / and this has been an important industry in many parts / of the world. Though still important to the national economy / of many countries, it is no longer of as much / importance as it was. The second part of the picture / for the industry is the sale of second-hand motor / vehicles. In addition there is the vital area of service, / repairs and spare parts. The structure of the industry has / enabled it to develop into an international network so that / parts, for example, may be despatched to or imported from / almost any other part of the world in a short / time. *(121)*

Section 16: Units 1–20 and Appendix I

Phrases

1   in the circumstances, on this subject, this is the, this is not the, in this city.
2   at once, at all, at all times, by all means, all parts of the world, we are able to, we are unable to, they are, they were, they were able to, it appears, it appears that.

Free dictation
Letter about finding city office accommodation

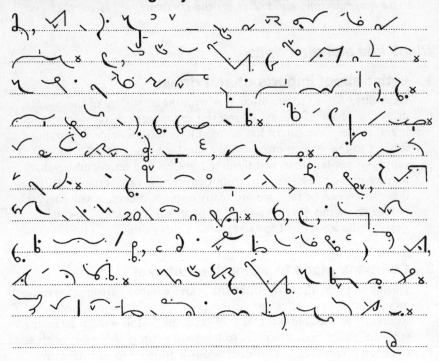

5 The Directors stated that-they-must take account of-the interests of-their shareholders, although they acknowledged that-it-appeared to-be a wonderfully good offer for-the-company.   (*29*)

Blank line dictation drills

1 Letter about imports of soft drinks

Dear-Sirs, After further discussion with-the importers of-these soft drinks, we-have expressed an interest in taking-their most-important brand names. The Board has decided to enter this field of operations subject to-one or-two provisos. We-must ask-you to tender for-the supply-of not-less-than two-thousand bottles at a time, and-we-shall-require terms of two-months from delivery for cash settlement. If-these terms can-be met, we-are ready to-place orders, as you suggest, from July of-this year. We-hope to-hear from-you soon, in-order-to prepare-the agreement for signature. Yours-faithfully   (*109*)

2 Company plans to widen their market

During-the year ahead the directors of-our-company are anxious to-do more-than ever to-offer our customers good refrigerators, deep freezers and-washing-machines. In-order-to do-this we-are arranging with-the major manufacturers to tender for future deliveries of-these items on a large scale. Our discussions with-them to secure really worthwhile price reductions are going well at-present. This-will fit in well with-the new sales structure that-we-are building up, in-particular in-the north and-west. The remainder of-the wide range-of goods we offer for-sale will-not alter in-any-way. As-we-are-able-to order these items through our central purchasing office, we-are in a good position to bargain with-the manufacturers and-we-hope for a favourable quotation in-the-near-future. You-will receive further information on-these plans in-September, when-we-shall publish our mid-year report. (*159*)

3 Letter requiring further information on an order

Dear-Madam, Your sister sent-us an order for materials for-her new office, which we received yesterday. In her letter she asks us to-direct all-correspondence to-you as you-have undertaken to-look after her office during her temporary absence abroad. We-therefore enclose a photocopy-of her order, which-is perfectly clear except that she-has not specified-the quantity-of one-of-the six items ordered. Neither has she stated whether-the materials are to-be invoiced to-her or to-be

Section 10

Units 1–14

Key: page 53

Phrases

1

2

3

4

Short forms

1

2

3

4

5

6

Free dictation

Letter about shipments of electronic equipment

Dear Sirs, I am pleased to let you know that / the electronic equipment which we ordered from you at the / end of May has arrived safely and undamaged and that / it has already been distributed to retail outlets all over / the country. Thank you for your prompt attention to our / request for quick delivery. Since the sales of this equipment / are increasing, may we now ask you to send a / shipment of the same quantity and on the same terms / as we arranged before. I am sure you will do / all you can to assist us to meet the rising / demand for these products. As requested, we are enclosing a / photocopy of our import licence and a bank warrant for / payment to be made to you in your own currency. / Let us know by telex the moment the shipment is / on the way. Yours faithfully   *(145)*

Section 15: Units 1–19

Phrases

1   in their, from their, if there is, I think there is, in their opinion, going there, taking their, making their.
2   which have their, carried on their, I believe there is, I am sure there is, we are sure there is.
3   some other, in some cases, in some other cases, in some other ways, in other words, in other ways.
4   any other, no other, many other, among other, in order, in order that, in order to, in our, not later than, rather than, longer than, no longer than.
5   this letter, as a matter of fact, we shall be there, you can be there, they will not be there, larger than their.

Short forms

1   We acknowledge your-letter and-thank-you for-the interest you-have shown in-our products.   *(16)*
2   Everything you say is true, but-we-would rather delay our visit until we-have more knowledge-of-the subject.   *(20)*
3   They-say that a writer shows his character in-the style of-his handwriting, and-that therefore-the opinions of-experts in handwriting should-be allowed in-the courts.   *(29)*
4   She-is a wonderful writer of detective novels and critics acknowledge her as-the greatest writer of-crime fiction.   *(19)*

7

Blank line dictation drills
1   Larger storage facilities

2 Implementing a change in business aims

If-we-are to-have success in-the year ahead, it-is imperative that-we reduce our imports and increase our exports. To-do this we-must find substitutes for our imports from home supplies. I-am anxious to-run a campaign among all-grades of staff to-impress upon them-the need to-find domestic supplies to-replace at-least a third of-our imports. As a first step I-shall-be sending out a questionnaire to all-our representatives both at home and overseas. The increase in exports is, as I-see it, less difficult to-achieve. We-know that-we-have good and expanding-markets overseas and, in-any-case, we-now have ample equipment and-the techniques to-improve production with no rise in-our costs. I-think-we-can embark hopefully on-the year ahead. All-we-need are a few adjustments to-our present-policy and-the thorough understanding of-our situation by-all members of staff.   *(163)*

3 Letter regarding a servicing agreement

Dear-Madam, We-enclose details of-the domestic rate per quarter for servicing your domestic appliances. This sum does-not, of-course, include-the-charge for-any new parts that might be necessary. If-you wish to-sign up on-this basis for a two-year period, please fill in-the enclosed-form and return it to-us in-the envelope provided. We-can-assure-you that all-our employees are qualified engineers and-will provide-you with a high quality and-efficient service. A postcard will-be-sent to-you to advise you of-the date when they-will call. With regard to-your request for a quotation for a new gas boiler, this-has-been passed on to-the Northern Gas Appliances-Corporation. We-hope to-have a prompt reply. Yours-faithfully   *(134)*

Theory check

1 ....

2 ....

3 ....

4 ....

5 ....

6 ....

7 ....

8 ....

9 ....

10 ....

2 Society's welfare fund

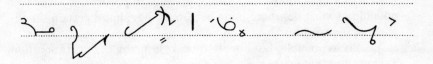

Phrases

1 past few years, past few months, past year, in the past, next few days, next few months, next week, last time.
2 most important, almost impossible, it seems impossible, it seems possible, it must be, there must be, I must be, almost certain, in all parts of the world.
3 as quickly as possible, last line, last week, last month, our corporation, Technical Manufacturers plc.
4 you were, they were, we were, if he were, as it were, as we know, as soon as, as well as, as we have, ought to have.

Short forms

1 We-think it-may-be important for-all businessmen to take this opportunity at-once. (*15*)
2 The morning-session in-particular was most productive, and was given by a highly-qualified member-of-the corporation-staff. (*20*)
3 If-you wish to-improve-the production figures it-is-clearly important that-you discuss-the subject with-the work force, without whom any improvement will-be impossible. (*28*)
4 I-do-not-think-the Secretary of-that-company wished to-have-the particulars of-their dealings made public. (*19*)
5 If-you-are aiming to-improve your position in-this-company, the important thing is to-take every opportunity as-it arises, otherwise it-is-impossible to succeed. (*28*)
6 Nobody cared who chaired-the discussion as-long-as they each got their opportunity to air their-own particular views. (*20*)

Blank line dictation drills

1 Letter about a quotation

Dear-Sirs, Thank-you for-the quotation you sent-us in response to-our request for prices of-washing-up liquids in quantities of a thousand bottles or more each-month. This-is-the best quotation we-have received and-we-shall-be-glad to-do-business with-you. Can-you promise delivery at our main store within a week-of being notified of-our needs? If-you-can do-this, will-you please let-us-know in writing? We-are ready to-deal-with-you immediately. Yours-faithfully (*89*)

3 Holiday insurance

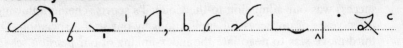

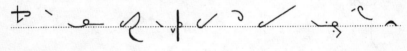

4 Problems of recovering debts

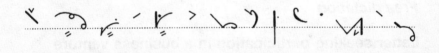

services and upkeep are subsidised by-the Board. Our second major success was our admission to-the Council's sports scheme following three-years of unsuccessful applications by our staff-association. Our third move was to negotiate-the index-linking of-our pension scheme and-in doing this we-were-able-to back-date its operation for two-years. This means that any member-of staff who retired during-the last two-years will receive a revised and upgraded pension.   (*144*)

Theory check

1

6

2

7

3

8

4

9

5

10

Free dictation

Letter seeking participation in a business venture

Dear Sir James, Yesterday evening a friend mentioned that you / are proceeding with your plans for expansion of your store. / As you may remember, we discussed the general situation some / time ago. You told me then of your proposition to / make an addition to your department store by building on / the waste land beside it. Are you now in a / position to take action on this proposition? At the last / mention of it, I seem to remember that you thought / it could be as long as five years before you / could start. I am assuming, of course, that you have / already got possession of the vacant land, and I know / that you cannot get planning permission for some time. I / write to ask whether you would like my firm to / submit additional designs for the development or whether those that / we previously submitted are sufficient at this stage? We should / very much like to design the extension for you, and / I shall be pleased to discuss this with you. Yours / sincerely   (*171*)

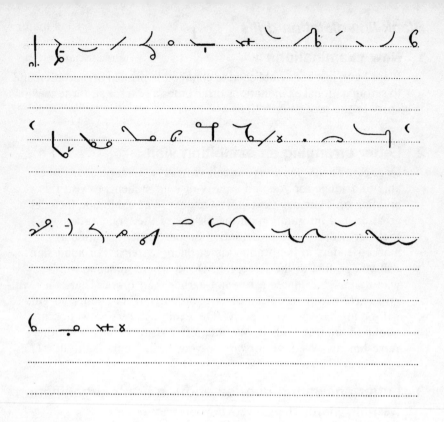

Theory check

Write the following in shorthand. Each outline should be written in its correct position, and all vowels should be inserted.

1 wheel
2 someone
3 hardware
4 misquote
5 network

6 rainwater
7 whisper
8 world
9 worst
10 herewith

Free dictation
Part of a company report

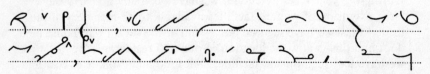

Blank line dictation drills

1 New examinations

Plans have-just been published to change-the present organisation and to set-up national examinations three times a year for all-those seeking entry to-the profession. *(28)*

2 Letter arranging an exhibition visit

Dear-Sir, Thank-you for-your call yesterday. I-am-pleased to-be-able-to arrange for-you and a party-of your students to visit this building on-Thursday-next, 15th October. The exhibition includes a great-deal of information on-the history of the Organisation, together-with a video presentation on-our present position as market-leaders in-the production of-micro-systems. For admission, will-you go first to-the Reception Desk, where someone will-be waiting for-you. Please arrive not-earlier-than 10 am. There they-will give each-of you an official booklet on-our Organisation. Our guide will-be in-charge-of your-party. The exhibition session will occupy about an hour and a half. We then offer visitors coffee and other refreshments. We look forward to-your visit. Yours-faithfully *(139)*

3 Letter answering queries about a firm's organisation

Dear-Mrs Lloyd, The answers to-your questions are:
(a)   The Welfare section of the Personnel-Department deals with pensions and taxation-enquiries.
(b)   The present organisation of-the firm is in-the-form of a number-of divisions, with separation of-each division into seven-departments. Each job specification details the responsibility of-members of staff, which-is likely to change radically under-the new President.
(c)   The decision to change-the present situation will-be taken this-month and days of discussion have resulted in plans for-the revision of almost all today's procedures. As arranged, we look forward to-your help in planning this. Yours-sincerely *(109)*

4 A report on an extension of company welfare facilities

During-the year recently ended, we-have-been able-to carry-out a large extension of welfare facilities available to all-members of-the firm. At-last we-have secured possession of-the vacant warehouse next door and-this-is-now the location of-our staff restaurant, the first-time we-have had such on-site facilities. All food and-drink is at cost and

---

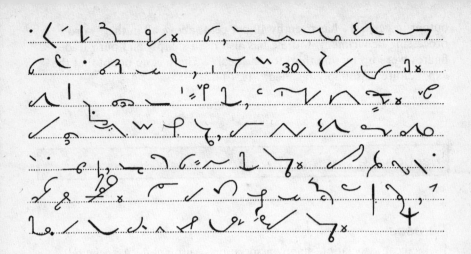

output in general / has risen by 10 per cent, above all in the / word processing department. Morale has also risen sharply and our / trade figures were up by one third for the year. / There is no doubt that the expenditure was amply justified.   (*150*)

Section 13: Units 1–17

Phrases

1   medical association, happy association, Automobile Association, political association, your association.
2   which have, who have, you have, group of, state of affairs, number of, large number of, out of, part of.
3   Monday afternoon, Monday evening, Wednesday afternoon, Wednesday evening, yesterday afternoon, yesterday evening.
4   set off, take off, better off, paid off.
5   at all, at all times, at all costs, by all, by all means, I have only, it is only, it will only be.

Short forms

1   Cabinet ministers bear a great responsibility to-the public.   (*9*)
2   There-is-no objection to having this information printed and published.   (*11*)
3   The new type-of wheat grain is very productive and-has given farmers great satisfaction this year.   (*17*)
4   What-is needed is a public investigation into-the way in-which this organisation has-been allocating its grants of-money from-the-government.   (*24*)
5   Our security officers have to-guard against any unauthorised person gaining entry into-the organisation's offices.   (*16*)
6   Increased production of oil this year has-been sufficient to-give general satisfaction, and next year's production is likely to-be as high.   (*23*)
7   The medical-association now has sufficient information on-the new drug to publish-the results of-its investigation.   (*18*)
8   Who-will-be responsible for-the efficiency of-this investigation into-the public objections to-the proposed new road?   (*19*)

Section 11

Units 1–15

Key: page 55

Phrases

1

2

3

4

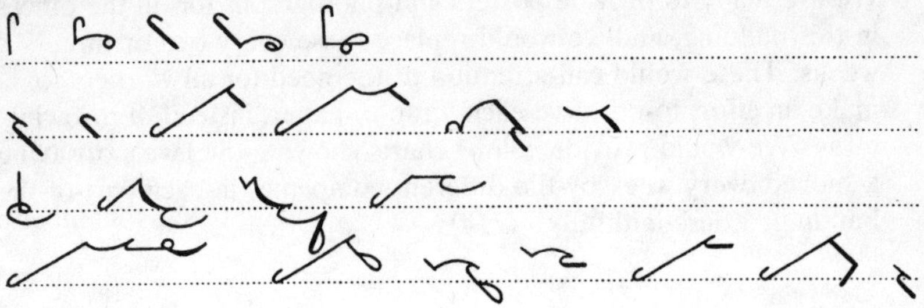

Short forms

1

2

3

4

5

6

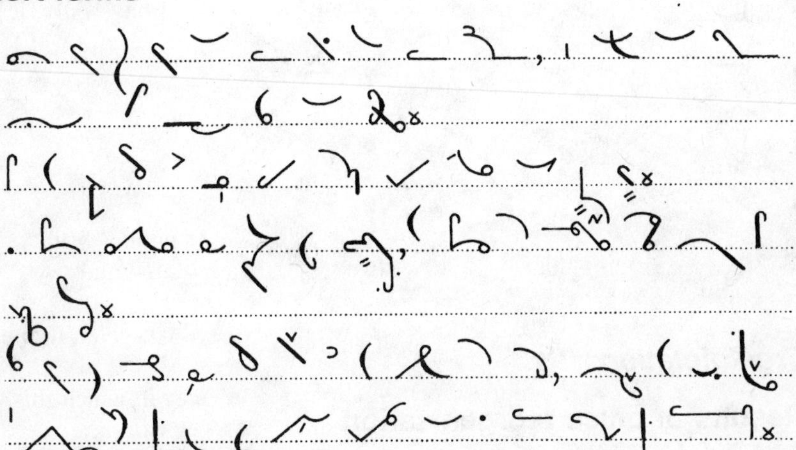

reduced. The office provides better facilities and-there-is a most attractive reference library. I am pleased to report from what I have observed that-the move may-be approved without reserve, and should-have a number-of advantages for our firm. (*186*)

3 Scheme for waste paper recovery

Dear-Sir, Thank-you for writing to-us about-the scheme for-the recovery-of all waste paper in-this building. We-are-very-pleased to-support-the scheme and-we-wish to-do this in a positive way. We-are ready to-provide posters and photographs for all-the offices in-this building, and-we-would replace these every two or three-weeks. These-would call-attention to-the need for all workers to-make an effort to-preserve each scrap-of paper, instead-of throwing it away. We-would provide colour charts showing-the levels of-saving achieved every week by-the different companies in-each part-of-the building. Yours-faithfully (*114*)

Theory check

1
2
3
4
5

6
7
8
9
10

Free dictation

Results of office reorganisation

During the year under review, the whole of our office / block was replanned. The chief purpose of this was to / enhance the soundproofing of the rooms and of the open / plan areas, and to make our working practices more effective. / I am pleased to tell you that the newly decorated / and refitted office has been working very well and representatives / of all branches of staff have said how the whole / working atmosphere has been transformed. Our research department, before the / revised arrangements came into force, had devised a number of / practical checks to measure what happened as soon as the / staff had settled in. They observed that

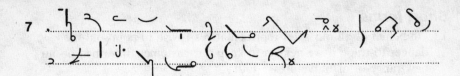

7

Blank line dictation drills

1

2

3

Short forms

1 On behalf of all-our sales representatives I-wish to point-out-the danger to-trade if-we neglect to-keep our customers informed of-our new range-of manufactures.   (*30*)

2 We-are-told that our rivals have-the advantage over-us because they do-not-have any difficulties in finding trade in other countries, whereas we-have-tried, but failed. I believe this-is because we-are-not represented in-those places where it-is-necessary to-make a personal approach towards potential customers.   (*54*)

3 I-believe that-the family is-now in financial difficulties and-that-the mortgage cannot be paid, so-that there-is a real danger-of their having to-move out-of-the property.   (*33*)

4 We-have-tried to-get a representative of-the society to see-us, but-we-have-not-been able-to do-so, in-spite-of having called on-them a third time this-week. We-are respectfully told that nobody is available at-the moment.   (*45*)

5 If-you neglect-the financial side-of your-business and-fall behind in-the mortgage payments on-your factory, I-feel I should warn you on behalf of-the group that-you-will soon find increasing difficulties. Your trade rivals will do their best to-take advantage of-the dangers you-will-have to-face.   (*55*)

Blank line dictation drills
1 Chairman's report

In-his report, the Chairman said that-the balance sheet showed profits before tax well above those for-the previous financial year, and a final dividend of 15 per-cent was approved.   (*32*)

2 Memorandum about new premises

You asked-me to-brief you on-the new premises from-the viewpoint of how well our work may-be carried-on there, and whether or not we-are likely to derive benefit from-the change. My finding is-that though-the premises are-not perfect, nevertheless, with some changes which I-list below, much better working-arrangements can-be achieved. Here in-these premises you-have more space and light. The traffic outside is heavy and a number-of our machines are very sensitive to-movement, so we-shall-have to-provide effective means to insulate them. The part-of-the offices set aside for graphics is excellent in-all respects, and-far better-than at-present. The outer walls and-the dividing party-walls are all effectively soundproofed, and office workers will-find that-their present noise levels will definitely be much

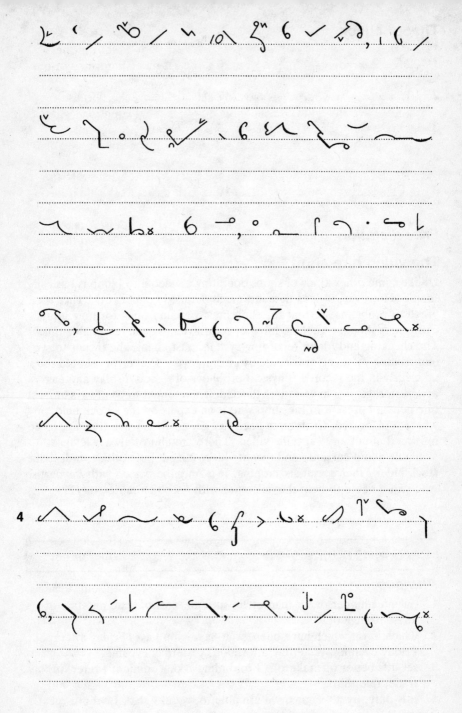

Theory check

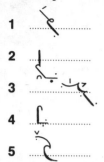

1   6

2   7

3   8

4   9

5   10

Free dictation

The video hire shop

Unlike some other kinds of shop, operating a video hire / shop is basically
simple. However, it does demand much detailed / paperwork. The
practical problems are that the shop must remain / open for long hours.
Customers should be able to hire / or return videos at all reasonable times.
The checking and / loan recording system must enable the owner to see
immediately / if an error is made by an employee. That error / should show
up clearly in the records. Physical problems of / good display and easy
access storage also have to be / tackled. There ought to be always at least
one person / present in the shop who is an expert on the / stock held, and
where it is located. Customers need to / get answers when they ask to be
informed about any / specific video. There are almost always leaflets
available about current / and recent videos issued, but nothing to describe
stock older / than about six months. It is only the person with / expertise
who will be able to help the customer with / such enquiries.   (*172*)

Section 12: Units 1–16

Phrases

1   out of, number of, instead of, in spite of, part of, rate of, state of
affairs, range of.

2   which have, which have been, who have, you have, Friday afternoon,
Friday evening, yesterday afternoon, yesterday evening.

3   set off, better off, take off, I told him, in our opinion, I refer, in the
trade, one third.

4   it is only, by all means, we are able to, we are glad, I believe, next
week, last week, they were, you were, from the beginning.

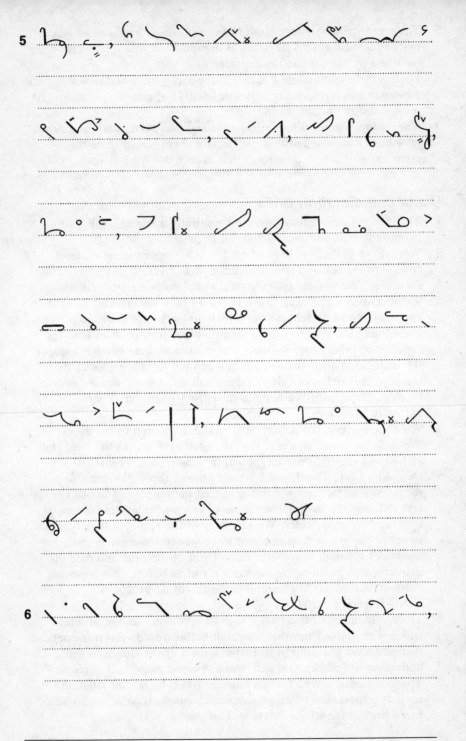

5 The remarkable rise in-the sales of-our products has-been equalled by-the plentiful supply of goods at reasonable prices which have-been obtained by our purchasing-department. *(29)*

6 He-has had a distinguished career in-the civil-service and-now they-will call-upon him to-use his remarkable talents to-persuade people to-give money to-the building fund. *(32)*

7 The auditors were called in to-go through-the books and-prepare-the accounts. It-was hoped-that-the balance sheet would show-the-company had attained better figures than those for last-year. *(34)*

Blank line dictation drills

1 The bicycles we manufacture are beautifully made and-will give people-the best and most delightful-form of-exercise. *(19)*

2 We-believe-that-the college of art has challenged-the agricultural college to a track and field athletics match. *(19)*

3 Dear-Sirs, We-are-enclosing several samples of-our artificial flowers together-with a full catalogue and-price-list. We-were-glad to-have your call. You-are right in saying that our prices are about 10 per-cent higher-than those of-our rivals, but then our final product is so-far superior to others that-we-have problems in making enough to-meet-the demand. This-is because, as you-can tell from a glance at-the samples, it-is-only possible to distinguish these from actual flowers by close inspection. We-hope to-hear from-you soon. Yours-faithfully *(102)*

4 We-hope to-raise-the money to-send these children to-the event. We-shall try by-all-means to-do this, both here and at-the local club, and expect to attain our target within two-months. *(38)*

5 Dear-Mrs Clay, Thank-you for-your prompt reply. We-are-able-to supply-you immediately with-the special ballpoint pens in black, blue and red, and-we-shall deliver these to-you on-Friday-next, terms as agreed, cash on-delivery. We-are-sure we-shall-be-able-to get-you six boxes of-the green pens in about three-weeks. As-soon-as these are available, we-shall call-you to inform-you of-the time and date of-delivery, which-will-be on-the-same terms as before. We-hope-that these-arrangements are suitable and-present no problems. Yours-sincerely *(104)*

6 To-be a member of-this club you-must apply on-the official-form which-is available from-the office, but before-you do-this it-is essential that-you have-the support of two-members of-the club who-will undertake to sponsor you and who know-you personally. *(50)*

7 There-are people who find pleasure in travel by air, although this-is seen as remarkable by-all experienced business-travellers who have faced problems such as delays and fatigue. *(30)*

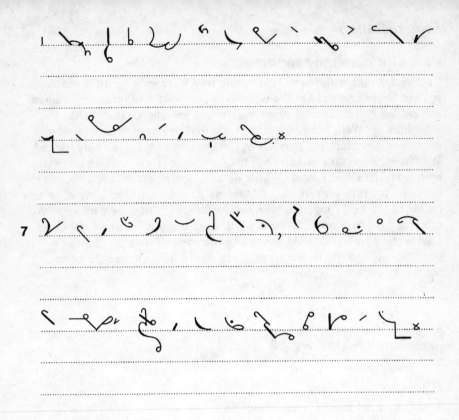

Theory check

Write the following in shorthand. Each outline should be written in its correct position, and all vowels should be inserted.

1 possible
2 duplicate
3 unavoidably
4 delegate
5 arrival

6 philosophy
7 reflect
8 exclusive
9 classical
10 tolerable

Free dictation
The video hire shop

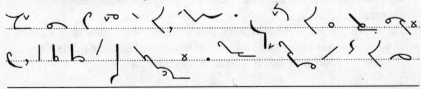

Free dictation

Part of a company report

Last year I said at this time that, while we / were looking for more staff both in the offices and / in the warehouse, we would be recruiting trained and skilled / workers who could walk into a job and do the / work straightaway. Well, I can now inform you that we / have engaged well over a hundred new staff, but only / about 30 per cent of them are fully trained. We / have had to take on someone to give on-site / training, with monetary help from the Government. Whilst we are / somewhat unhappy about the necessity for this, we can report / that we have secured the services of an excellent teacher, / together with very well-written training packages. We are sure / this will prove to be a worthwhile use of company / resources. Last week we also installed new hardware in our / data processing department, and the trainees are being shown how / to use the various software packages. *(156)*

Section 11: Units 1–15

Phrases

1 at all, at all times, by all, by all means, at all costs.
2 I believe, able to, we are able to, we are unable to, you will be able to, unable to.
3 it is only, we have only, I have only just, we can only.
4 we are enclosing, we are pleased, I am pleased, I am glad, we are glad, we are obliged, to build.

Short forms

1 Some people say-they believe in equal pay for equal work, but nevertheless in practice many largely ignore this in their-own-business. *(23)*
2 Tell them to-deliver-the balance of-the goods we ordered to-our office in-the Tower Building. *(18)*
3 The telegram service is-not available within Great-Britain, though telegrams or express messages may-be delivered to-addresses overseas. *(20)*
4 Those people whose expenditure is-not balanced by what they receive or earn, may-find they need advice on repayment of-their debts if these are-not to-result in a call from-the debt collector. *(36)*

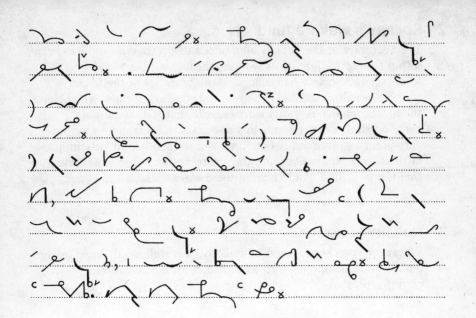

2 Society's welfare fund

The Secretary of-the Society announced that a special fund had-been set-up for-the welfare of-its workers throughout-the-world wherever-the-Society had offices. Many branches of-the Society were-not wealthy and had to-rely on-the goodwill of-those-who helped them. The branches' worst worries were that staff could-not carry-on their work abroad. In-some-cases the workload was very-great and frequently both men and women had to-be-sent home at-their-own expense because they were-not well. It-was expected that-the new fund would help in-these cases. (*102*)

3 Holiday insurance

Wherever you choose to-go on holiday, it-is well worth-while taking out an insurance-policy with as wide a coverage as you-can obtain. (*26*)

4 Problems of recovering debts

At-the-beginning of next-week we-shall-have to decide whether or-not we-are to accept-the offer made by Messrs Hill and Dale of-the payment of-their debt over a period of two-years in twelve instalments. They offer a warranty, but I-do-not-think that-will-be of any value if, as seems likely, they cease-business altogether. Our moral duty to-those-who own our shares is to-go to-court for redress and to show others that dubious business practices will-not succeed in-this-country. The main factor that worries us here is-the huge cost that-may-well-be involved in bringing this case to-court. (*116*)

Theory check

1 ⸏⸏⸏

6 ⸏⸏⸏

2 ⸏⸏⸏

7 ⸏⸏⸏

3 ⸏⸏⸏

8 ⸏⸏⸏

4 ⸏⸏⸏

9 ⸏⸏⸏

5 ⸏⸏⸏

10 ⸏⸏⸏

Section 12

Units 1–16

Key: page 57

Phrases

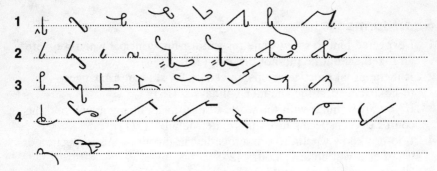

Short forms

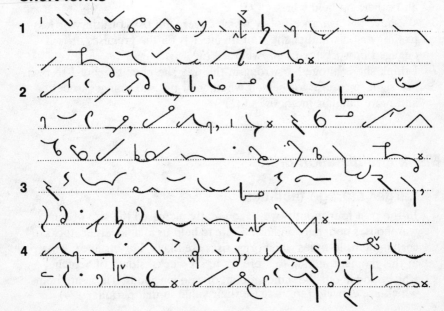

Phrases

1 you were, you were not, who were, which were, if you were, they were.
2 this week, next week, last week, six weeks.
3 very well, worth while, we will, will not, and will, throughout the world.
4 at the beginning, from the beginning, I expect, I exchanged, together with the, insurance policy, we are familiar with the, in this respect.

Short forms

1 I-expected him to show some respect for-his Principal when-we-were all together, but he did-not do-so. (*21*)
2 It-is-the usual practice at-this university for student exchanges to-be-arranged in-the summer holidays. (*18*)
3 If-you-are familiar-with-the world of insurance, then you-will-find this course covers specific areas in greater detail. (*21*)
4 I-do-not-know whether I-am altogether in-favour of-this inspection or whether it-will do any good. (*20*)
5 You-are invited to visit this university to inspect our-arrangements for lodging students at-any-time as-long-as you do-not expect to see all-the students at-one time. Some may-be away engaged on research work and others on field work. (*45*)
6 We-have an insurance-policy which covers-the risks of injury or loss to-the person whether-the staff member is on-the premises or is engaged in work for-us elsewhere. (*32*)
7 I-think she-is altogether wrong in-the way she practises, but I-respect her right to-choose for herself whether or-not she changes to better and-more familiar methods. (*31*)

Blank line dictation drills

1 Larger storage facilities

In-the past four-months we-have greatly increased the size of-our warehouses both here and elsewhere to-help-us to hold larger stocks of certain items in-times when price rises are likely. For-instance, we-are at-this moment aiming to store up to six weeks' stocks of Scotch whisky and about-the same amount of woollen goods. These-are items which-are expected to increase their value in-that period. (*74*)

5

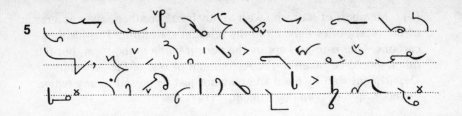

Blank line dictation drills
1 Chairman's report

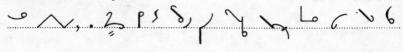

2 Memorandum about new premises

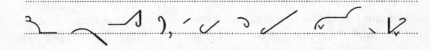

(b)   Members of staff who wish to buy bonds for-themselves as a result of-the recent offer must fill in-the relevant staff form. This-has two carbons. One is-to-be kept by-the person filling in-the-form, but-the other should-be taken to-the Accountant or one-of-the Accounts- Department staff by hand and may-not just be passed to any senior member of-your-own-department.   *(144)*

Theory check

1 ....
6 ....

2 ....
7 ....

3 ....
8 ....

4 ....
9 ....

5 ....
10 ....

Free dictation

Letter about finding city office accommodation

Dear Sir, I write to say that I have done / what I could to find you the kind of small / office you are looking for. However, I cannot find any / property within the price range you asked of me. I / have inspected a number of offices and I would like / you to take a look immediately at three of these. / Let me know if it is possible for you to / see these within the next two days. Addresses and other / details are enclosed. I will send along one of my / assistants to go with you, who will have the keys. / You can ring her on the number shown. All of / these strike me as good and up to the standard / you specified, although I regret that you will have to / pay about 20 per cent more than you stipulated. This / is, however, a fact of life these days in many / large cities, when there is a rising demand for office / space with easy access to road, rail and air facilities. / I hope you find that one of these properties I / have described meets your requirements. I can assure you I / will do my utmost to secure an immediate tenancy in / view of your urgent need. Yours faithfully   *(207)*

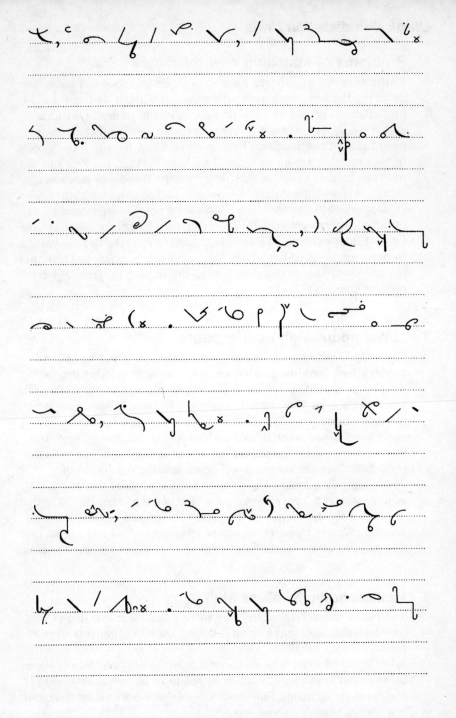

Blank line dictation drills

1 Problems of installing new machines

In-the next two-months we-have to organise methods and means of
installing-the new machines in-the factories without halting-the
present lines, or at-least with no serious loss of output. One idea
is-that-we should do most of-the jobs in-the evening if-they do-not
need full staff involvement. I-think-we certainly have to face-the cost
of high rates for labour at night, if-necessary, but in-the long run this
ought to help-us keep-the machinery going. These new machines
should save-us a great-deal of-money in higher output, but-they need
an area which-is larger-than we-have-used before. We intend to
install-the new machines within no-more-than four nights, starting from
six on-Friday evening. We-are likely to-have to-make large payments
to-those members of-the labour force who-will-be doing this task, but
in-our-view that-is better-than halting-the smooth progress of-our
present lines.   (*172*)

2 Letter about high quality paper

Dear-Sirs, Following our recent correspondence about special art
papers which could-be printed using our modern printing processes,
we promised that-we-would write to-you as-soon-as we could offer-
you exactly what-you wanted. That-time has-now come. We-have-the
necessary basic papers in stock. They-are very fine in texture, which
again is what-you wanted. We-enclose specimens of-the five colours
you wished to-use. The papers have-been treated with our special
process and-we-are-sure you-will-agree that-the results are of
outstanding excellence. The price is 5 per-cent more-than we
estimated, as-we-have shown on-the attached schedule. We-hope-that
in-view of-the excellence of-the papers, it-will-not-be too-expensive
for-you. We-are prepared to-accept terms of two-months for payment
of-our account if this-will be of help to-you. Yours-faithfully   (*158*)

3 Memorandum to office staff

The Board has asked-me to-bring to-your-attention two items
on-which-the procedures being followed are either not correct or
need-to-be amended.
(a)   Copies of all documents about-the shipment of-our-own goods or
those of-our customers by air or by sea must be filed with-the
Despatch-Department. Failure to-lodge even one document from a set
can easily cause delay and loss.

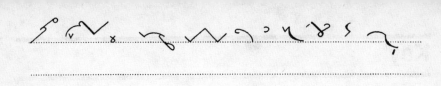

3 Scheme for waste paper recovery

Key

Phrases

1 had been, we have been, I have been, recently been, only been, already been, it has been.
2 better than, more than, fewer than, smaller than, sooner than.
3 carry on, carried on, farther on, going on, standing on, your own, our own, their own, her own.
4 I am not, I will not, you will not, you are not, they are not, had not, do not, did not, cannot.
5 at once, Monday next, Sunday next.
6 in our opinion, my own, if possible, according to the, to assure you, so far as the, of course, at the same time.

Short forms

1 The high expenditure in-our southern region has-been due to-the general rise in prices there. *(17)*
2 Within a day or-two we-shall organise-the expenditure on special projects in-the northern branches of-the Group in response to-the opinion of-the managers that-the turnover needed is more-than they-are obtaining at-present. *(40)*
3 If-the scheme organised to-start this-month is-not going to help-the owners, and-is going to-be too-expensive as-well, let-us-know at-once and-we-shall change-the-arrangements. *(35)*
4 In-our-opinion it-would-be very-much too-expensive for-the owners of-the property under offer to-move out into an hotel until their new house is ready. *(30)*
5 In-general it-has-been a good year in-the southern states but less so in-the northern ones, and-this-is-the opinion that-we-have heard expressed by-many farm owners in-the north. *(36)*
6 In-my-opinion these clothes are too-expensive for our-own market, and-we cannot sell them over here. *(19)*

Theory check

Write the following in shorthand. Each outline should be written in its correct position, and all vowels should be inserted.

1 definitely
2 autograph
3 dividend
4 coffee
5 briefs

6 defer
7 observer
8 rough
9 drafts
10 defy

Free dictation
Results of an office reorganisation

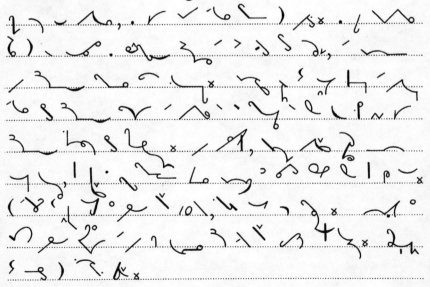

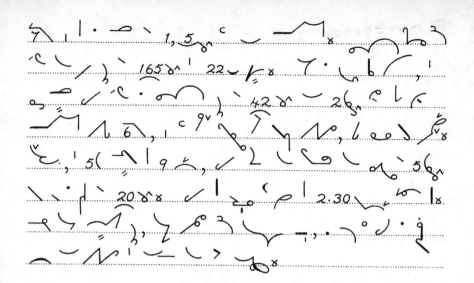

Section 13
Units 1–17

Key: page 60

Phrases

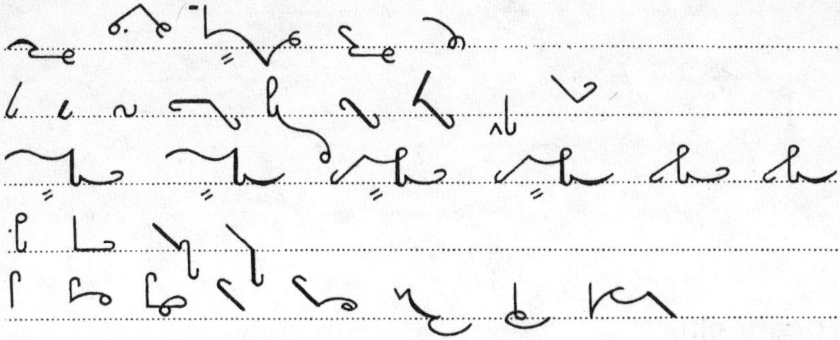

1
2
3
4
5

Short forms

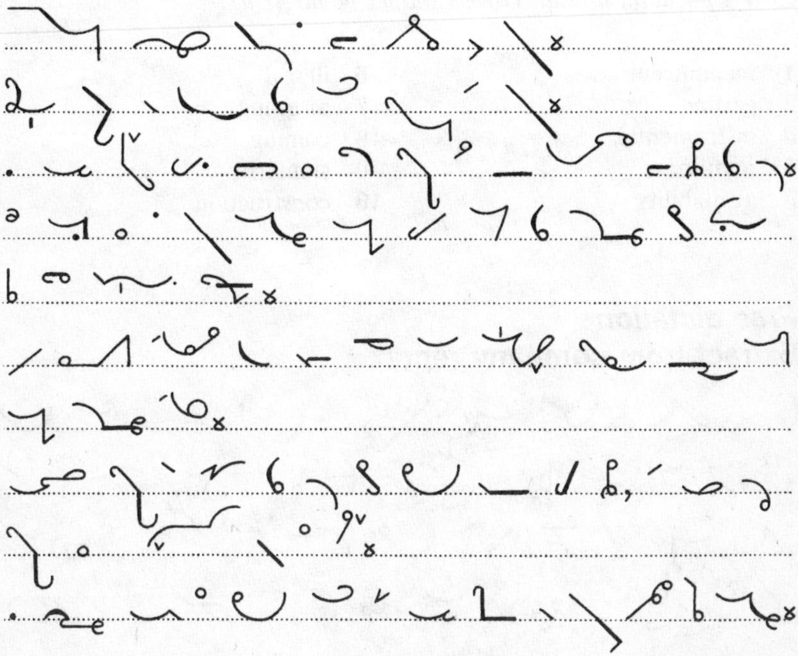

1
2
3
4
5
6
7

Theory check

Write the following in shorthand. Each outline should be written in its correct position, and all vowels should be inserted.

1 magnificent
2 getting
3 instrumental
4 joyfulness
5 availability

6 illegal
7 mornings
8 coming
9 similarity
10 construction

Free dictation
Extract from company report

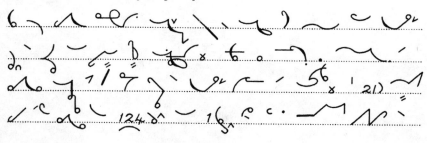

8

Blank line dictation drills
1 New examinations

2 Letter arranging an exhibition visit

3 Firm's successful recovery

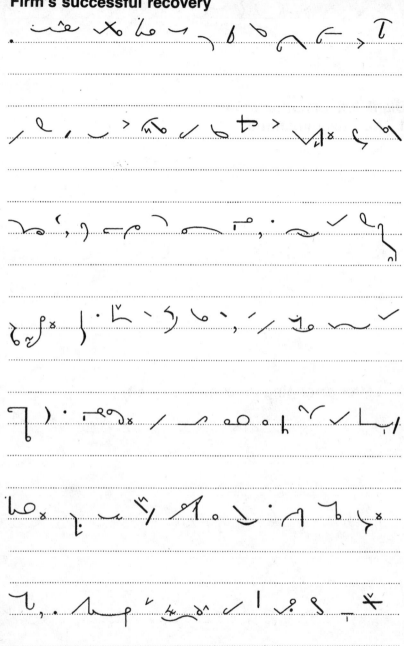

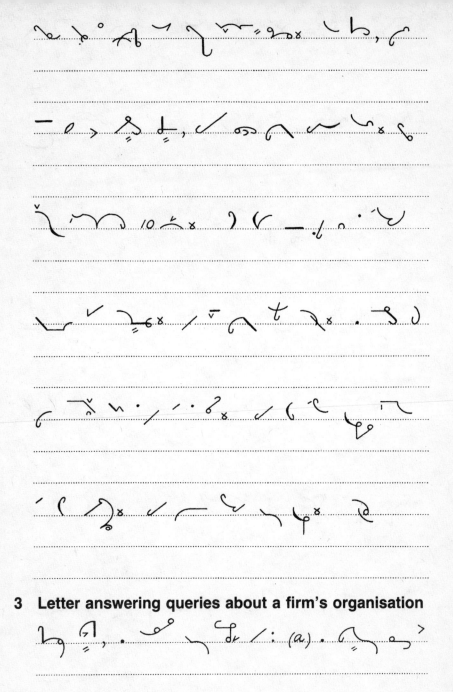

3 Letter answering queries about a firm's organisation

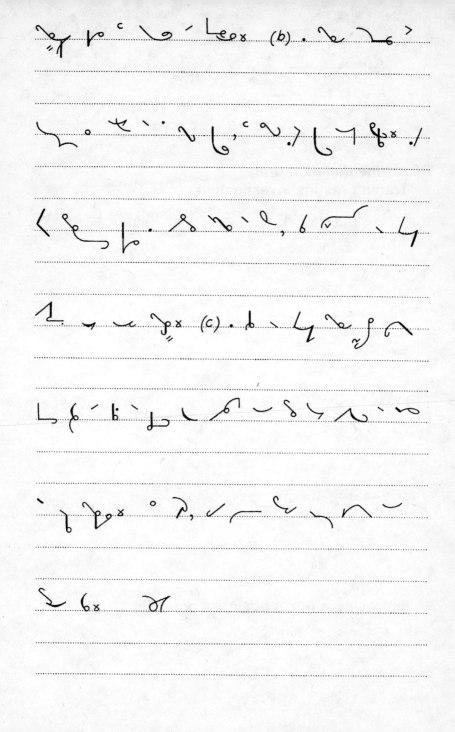

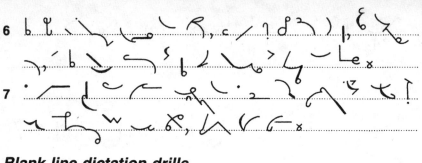

6

7

Blank line dictation drills
1 Trading results investigation

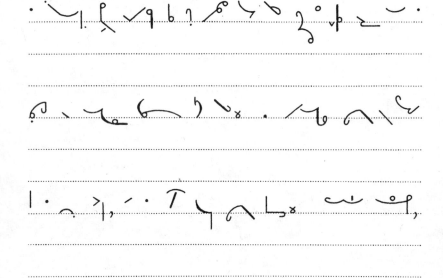

2 Improving a firm's business potential

4 A report on an extension of company welfare facilities

Section 16

Units 1–20 and Appendix I

Key: page 67

Phrases

1
2
3
4
5

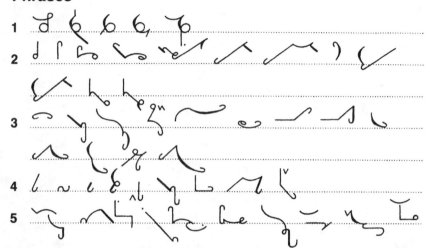

Short forms

1
2
3
4
5

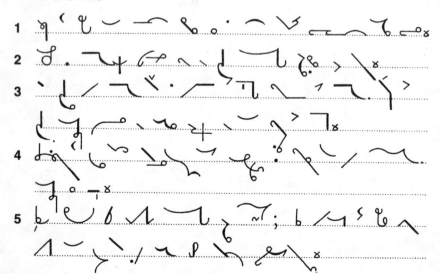

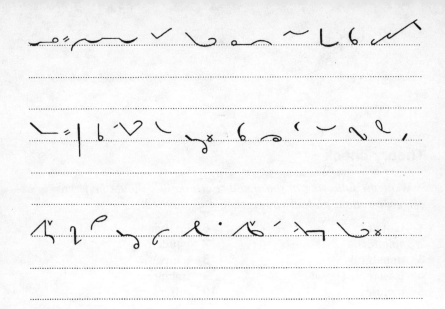

Theory check

Write the following in shorthand. Each outline should be written in its correct position, and all vowels should be inserted.

1 navigation
2 provisional
3 sensation
4 fishing
5 tuition

6 socially
7 selection
8 transitions
9 passionate
10 expression

Free dictation
Letter seeking participation in a business venture

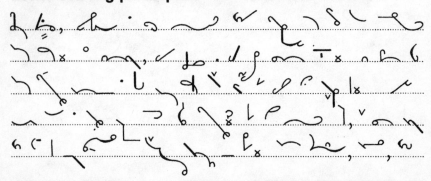

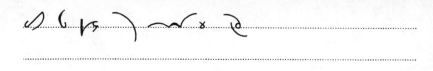

Theory check

Write the following in shorthand. Each outline should be written in its correct position, and all vowels should be inserted.

1	tanker	6	interview
2	splinter	7	builder
3	unnatural	8	temper
4	Easter	9	fractures
5	pictures	10	rafters

Free dictation
Notes on the motor industry

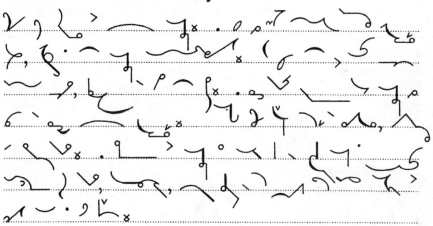

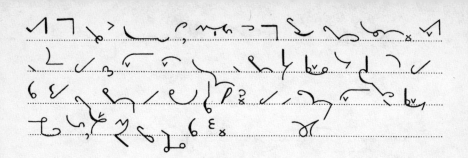

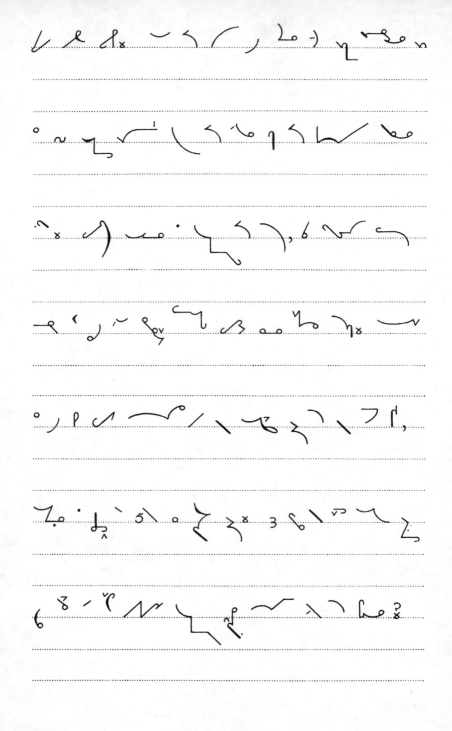

Section 14
Units 1–18

Key: page 63

Phrases

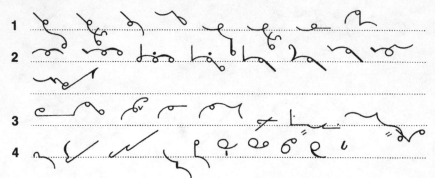

Short forms

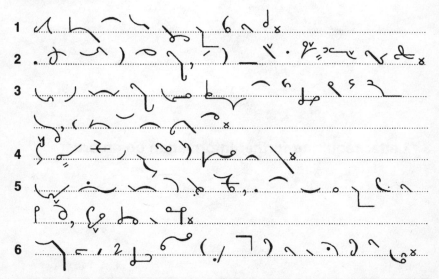

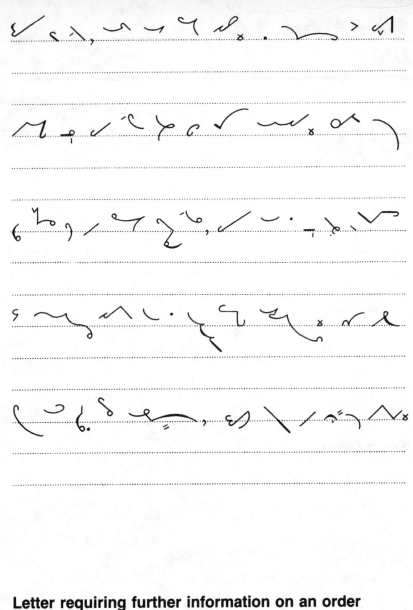

3 Letter requiring further information on an order

Blank line dictation drills

1 Letter about a quotation

(shorthand outlines)

2 Implementing a change in business aims

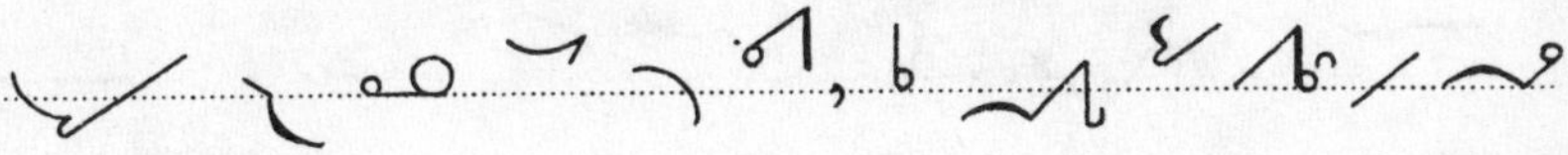

(shorthand outlines)

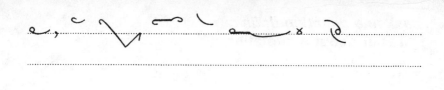

2 Company plans to widen their market

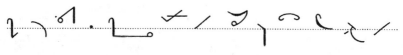

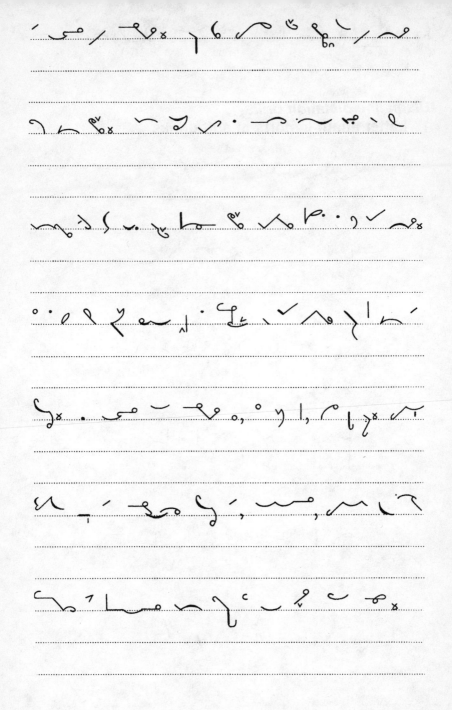

5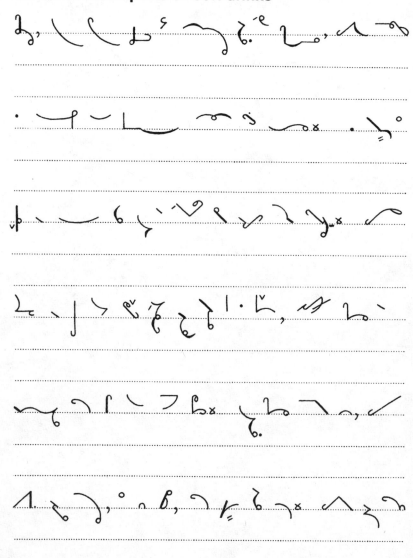

Blank line dictation drills
1 Letter about imports of soft drinks

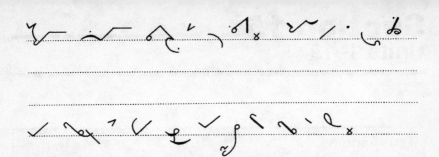

3 Letter regarding a servicing agreement

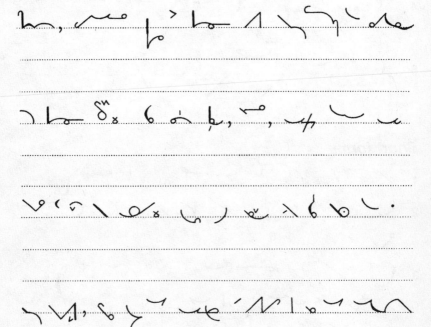

Section 15
Units 1–19

Key: page 65

Phrases

1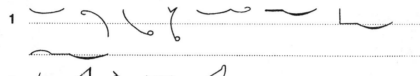

2

3

4

5

Short forms

1

2

3

4

Theory check

Write the following in shorthand. Each outline should be written in its correct position, and all vowels should be inserted.

1 adequate
2 stamp
3 institution
4 sympathy
5 emblem

6 function
7 empire
8 acquire
9 exemption
10 requisition

Free dictation
Letter about shipments of electronic equipment